# I Can't Find My Backpack!

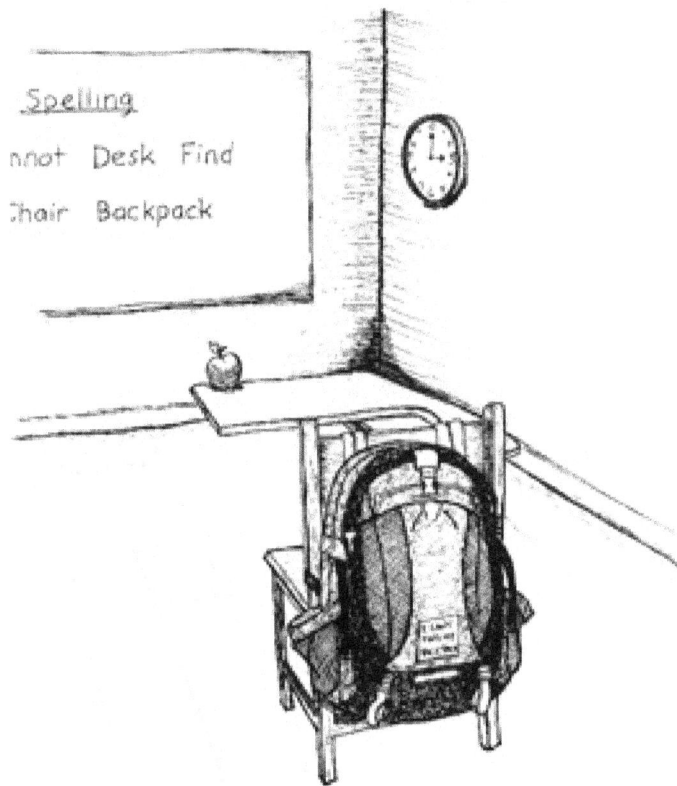

*Spelling*

*nnot  Desk  Find*

*hair  Backpack*

**Anecdotes and Poetry by Randall Fairley**
**Illustrated by Christina Faye Lee**

# Copyright

This book for your personal use only.  Thank you for respecting the hard work of this author.

*I Can't Find My Backpack* by Randall Fairley
Paperback    ISBN: 9781939687111
Ebook         ISBN: 9781939687081
BISAC POETRY / Subjects & Themes / Family
Library of Congress Control Number: 2016944744

First paperback publication by Fat Squirrel Publishing, San Marcos, TX
Date:  2016.
All rights are reserved.

# Randall Fairley

Mr. Fairley was an elementary school classroom teacher for eighteen years.  He retired from teaching in 2003 and lives in Vancouver, Washington with his wife and his two dogs. He spends his early mornings hanging out at the local coffee shop. He is a do-it-yourself home improvement enthusiast. Many of the selections in this book began with an actual incident in Mr. Fairley's classroom.

Some of Mr. Fairley's verses are simply imagination tied to childhood experience. A few are the result of reoccurring *mental funny-bone* moments. These are afflictions that Mr. Fairley has learned to live with, and he shares some of them with you in ***I Can't Find My Backpack.***

# Author Notes:

Background notes for some of those pieces are included. The anecdotes and comments concerning people, events, and conversations are taken from the author's eighteen years of teaching. The people and circumstances are composite in nature whose characteristics have been adapted conceptually. Visit www.grandpabradley.com or www.randallfairley.com

# Contents

Anecdotes and Poetry by
Randall Fairley

Illustrations by
Christina Faye Lee

# Grandpa Bradley

Grandpa Bradley
Combs his hairs
In a most peculiar way.
One lays north,
One lays south,
The third stands up all day.

# Anecdote: *I Can't Find My Backpack*

It was 3:00 PM. The classroom was in chaos. The buses would be leaving soon, and the children in my third grade classroom were scrambling to tidy up, pack up and get out the door.

Andrea approached me with a serious look on her face.

"Mr. Fairley, I can't find my backpack."

"Andrea, did you check the coat closet?"

Andrea bustled off to look in the coat closet. She returned and stated emphatically, "My backpack wasn't in the coat closet, Mr. Fairley."

I sent her to all of the likely places a third grader might lose track of a backpack. No luck. Each trip ended with the same message, "Mr. Fairley, my backpack wasn't___." Each time she repeated the message, the amused expression on her face grew. She was beginning to suspect that I was having fun. *I was.*

I finally gazed over toward Andrea's desk. Her desk was tidied and her chair was pushed in. I could tell that something was on her chair, down there beneath the desktop.

I chuckled to myself.

"**Mr. Fairley**!" Andrea interrupted.

Andrea was standing in front of me with her hands on her hips. Her eyes twinkled through the stern expression on her face.

"Mr. Fairley, my backpack was not in the Book Nook!"

"Why don't you check your desk area, again?" I suggested. Andrea replied, "Mr. Fairley, I've **already** checked my desk area!"

"It won't hurt to check again."

Less than a minute later, Andrea was standing in front of me again.  Her coat was on and backpack was draped across her shoulder.

"Mr. Fairley, my backpack was **on** my **chair**!"

We both laughed as she hurried off to see if her bus was still parked outside.

By the time I was ready to leave for home, I had decided to write something about Andrea and her backpack.

Something with rhyme, rhythm, and exaggeration.  Just for fun.  Just for me.  By 1:00 AM the following morning, I was putting the final touches on the selection entitled *I Can't Find My Backpack.*

It turned out that kids really like to read silly stuff with rhyme and rhythm, particularly when the subject matter relates to their life experience.

Good to know.   Especially, if you're a teacher.

I wish I had met Andrea fourteen years earlier.

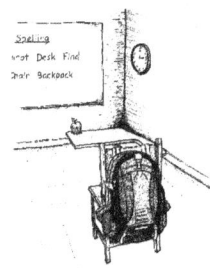

# I Can't Find My Backpack

I cannot find my backpack,
It's happened once again,
I laid it on my desk just now,
Beside my new blue pen.

I turned to talk to Courtney,
I told my teacher, "bye."
But when I turned to grab my pack,
My pack I couldn't spy.

Maybe Matt is hiding it
Behind his chair or desk.
Or maybe stuffed it up his shirt,
Against his hairless chest.

Jamie could have swallowed it,
Just one big gulp, then burp!
Or maybe Sarah's hiding it
Behind her purple skirt.

I told my teacher sadly that
My backpack, it was gone.
It was sitting by my new blue pen,
I hadn't left it long.

He turned and then he smiled at me,
And then he shook his head.

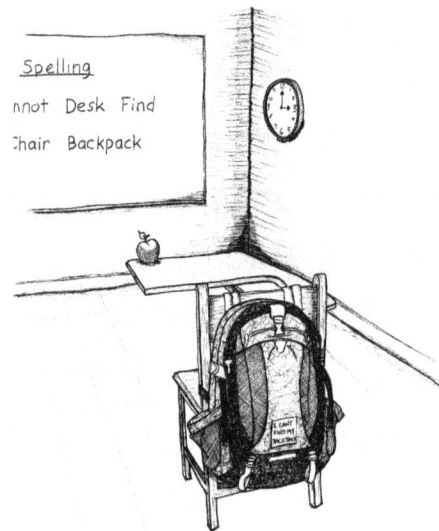

I bet he thinks I'm teasing him,
"Go look," is all he said.

That seemed a silly thing to say,
I'd looked most everywhere.
But wait!  What's that I see just now?
My backpack on my chair!

## What Someone Said To Wendy

I can't believe you hid my pencil,
Can't believe you took my chair!
I never thought you'd eat my apple,
Did you have to pull my hair?

I can't believe you stole my quarter,
Can't believe you chewed my gum!
I never dreamed you'd talk about me,
Did you really call me dumb?

I can't believe this way you're acting,
Can't believe you've been so rude!
I hope you come to school tomorrow
With a better attitude!

## Do, Dew, Due

Hairdo,
Mountain Dew,
Early morning dew.
Over due,
Past due,
Yucky, doggy doo!
Undo,
Make do,
Well now, whoop-ty-do!
I do, you do,
So much do, dew, due,
And doo!

# Bathroom Break

My friend's been gone,
A long, long time!
He really should be back.
He left five minutes after ten,
Just after morning snack.
The bathroom pass
Is on his desk,
His chair pushed neatly in,
And teacher's going on and on,
Like time and time again.

My friend's been gone
A long, long time!
I wonder why so long.
He could be feeling barfy sick,
There might be something wrong.
Or maybe he is fast asleep
Just sitting on the pot,
Or maybe swinging on the door,
He'll catch it if he's caught.

He might be up
To something foul.
He might be playing pranks,
Like clogging up the toilet bowl,
Or plugging up the sink.
Look, here he comes!
He smiles at me,
Then whispers in my ear,
"Don't go in there till Friday noon...
I've ruined the atmosphere!"

# Anecdote: *My Teacher's Breath*

I have a bad breath problem. I know it. The kids know it. I suppose a lot of people know it. Whenever one of my students kindly brought it to my attention, as in, "Mr. Fairley, your breath **smells bad!**" I explained it away as the result of my lunch menu. Finally, I decided to attack the issue with some rhyme and exaggeration. Our school principal loved it and insisted that it be read for the student body at the next school assembly. One of my kids was more than willing to take it on. Of course, it was a hit with the children. But I can tell you that no less than two teachers were observed by their students sporting red faces.

# My Teacher's Breath

My teacher's breath
Is worse than bad,
It's hard to understand,
How anything
Could be so foul,
Yet not be strictly banned.

It smells of things
Like broccoli,
Like onions, garlic, too,
Like vitamins
And medicine,
All mixed into a goo.

And when he speaks,
A cloud so green
Begins to fill the room,
And thickens with
Each word he breathes,
Till all is filled with gloom.
And classroom plants
Begin to droop,
And kids begin to choke.
This nasty fume
Inside our room
Is not a laughing joke.

And that is why
My friends and I,
To ease our greatest fear,
Get up each day
And go to school,
All dressed in scuba gear.

# Grandpa Bradley

Grandpa Bradley
Combs his hairs
In a most peculiar way.
One lays north,
One lays south,
The third stands up all day.

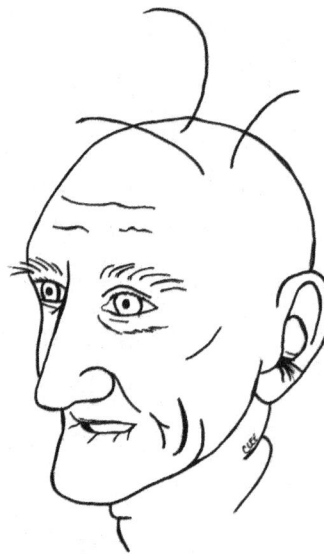

# Breath Mints

Each day the kids in classroom eight
Bring breath mints for their teacher.
An apple not, no flower pot,
Nor note, or painted picture.

For all the things kids usually bring,
To lavish on their teacher,
Could never help, not one small bit,
To make their classroom fresher.

# My Teacher Said

My teacher said,
"Please copy this,
Take care to make it neat.
The letters I must recognize,
So use correct technique."

My teacher said,
"Now do your math,
Your sums to ninety-nine.
My best advice is check it twice,
And you will do just fine."

My teacher said,
"Do question five,
Then look at question eight.
Record your thoughts about the plot,
Don't fail to punctuate."

My teacher said,
"It's time to rhyme,
Please jot a little line,
About a gnome, or home sweet home,
Or just the number nine."

My teacher said,
"I am concerned,
Your work you haven't done.
Please tell me why, if I may pry,
You haven't yet begun.

My teacher,
I will tell you why
I have not yet begun.
A pencil sharp, I need to start,
But sadly, I have none.

# Anecdote: *Why School's So Hard*

The typical crowd is around my desk.  Kids are trying to work their way to the center of the crowd.  So many important needs! Davy is small for his grade level.  He never seems to get any closer to me, but that's okay with him. He has plenty of company coming and going.  Suddenly, we are all aware of Davy's shrill, and somewhat loud laugh, followed by, "Hey, Mr. Fairley, looky where I am!" We all look and we all have a good laugh.

Davy's armpits and his knees are resting on the rim of the circular waste basket.  Everything in between is out of sight down inside the waste basket. Davy's face is beaming with delight.  It is clear that he thinks that this is just about as cool as school gets.  It was pretty cool!

# Why School's So Hard

Brittany's counting pinto beans,
She's making groups of ten.
But some end up inside her nose,
Some never seen again.

And Patrick's standing on his desk,
He kicks and swings and spins,
And imagines that his mortal foe,
Has fallen once again.

J. T.'s not sure what he should do,
Read, write, or draw a cow.
Or maybe play a game with John,
If John will teach him how.

And Sandra's standing by the sink,
A tissue in her hand.
She blows and blows until her nose
Sounds louder than a band.

Then Cooper yells, "Hey look at me.
Hey looky where I am!
Can you believe I'm sitting here
Inside the garbage can?"

I wonder how I'll do my math,
My sums to twenty-three,
Get better at my spelling words,
Read chapters two and three.

I wonder how I'll write a poem
And have it done today.
With all that's going on in here,
I think there's just no way.

# With Time (Trombone)

With time,
The sound I blow
Will grow,
I'm told,
With time
And much hard work.

The melody will glow,
The rhythm flow,
With time,
Blow by labored blow.

# Maybe

Maybe if I close my eyes,
Hold my breath,
And count to ten.
Maybe if I snap my fingers
Three times behind my back
And say a magic word.
Maybe if I touch my nose,
Wink my left eye,
And nod two times.
Maybe, just maybe,
This math problem
Will go away,
And I, at last,
Will go out to play.

# I Hope I Have It Straight!

I never thought I'd say it.
I swear it's really true.
I learned so much at school today,
So much I never knew.

I learned that six plus seven
Is nearly twenty-three,
That half of fourteen elephants
Makes eighteen wrinkled knees.

And frogs, you know are mammals,
And ostriches can fly.
Blue whales are really great big fish.
Hyenas really cry.

And did you know that Pluto
Is closest to the sun?
That Jupiter has thirteen moons?
That Saturn has just one?

I learned a lot today, mom.
But I am barely eight.
So many numbers, names, and things,
I hope I have it straight!

# Anecdote: *I Want To Go Home*

It seems there was at least one child, every year, at some point in the year, who really needed to go home...badly. One child in particular comes to mind. I'll call her Alicia. It started with a sore tummy. I showed some concern and then followed it with, "Let's see if it goes away. Be sure to let me know if it doesn't get better."

Well, Alicia was back in front of me in a few minutes, serious face in tow. "Mr. Fairley, my tummy still hurts."

Some more concern, this time followed with, "Lunch is coming up. Maybe you're just feeling hungry. Let's see how you feel after lunch."

"Ok."

Lunch was over and about 15 minutes had past. Alicia approached me again, with a pained look on her face, "Mr. Fairley, it **really** hurts. I need my mom!"

I need to clarify something here. Alicia didn't look like she was in pain, that is, not unless she was addressing me. Each time she went back to her seat the pain seemed to disappear. Been there before. And done that. So I just played along wanting to see where it would lead. Back to the story.

"We need to be really sure about this, Alicia. Mom is at work and she won't be happy if I send you home and the problem is a small problem." Alicia went back to her seat.

She was back shortly. "Mr. Fairley, my arm is hurting me now."
Alicia was a smart girl and she had realized that she was getting
nowhere with the *sore tummy* line.

Next came the headache line followed by a resumption of the
sore tummy line.

Finally, the day ended.

The following day, Alicia returned and we resumed the previous
day's tug of war.

Alicia won.

But, I had a good concept to couple with some exaggeration.

# I Want To Go Home

May I call my mom, please, Teacher?
There's so much I need to tell.
I have "owies" by the dozen,
And I don't feel all that well.

There's a sliver in my finger,
It's so small it's hard to see,
But I'm positive it's stuck there
By the way it's hurting me.

And my tongue is oh so tender
Cuz I bit it just today.
It's so hard to get my words out
When my mouth gets in the way.

My poor tummy, it feels funny
Like it can't make up its mind.
And I'm sure I'll need a barf bag
In a very little time.

My big toe has got a blister,
There's a pimple on my nose,
And the sunburn on my shoulders
Really smarts against my clothes.

May I call my mom, please, Teacher?
So, so much is wrong with me,
And I want to go home badly,
I won't last, I'm sure, till three!

# Anecdote: *The Queen of Dribble Drabble*

"Mr. Fairley, Sarah won't stop talking."
"Hum.  If you don't talk back to her, she'll probably stop talking."
"Mr. Fairley, we're not talking to her.  She's just talking... to no one."
**The Queen Of Dribble Drabble** does not employ exaggeration.
Well, very, very little.

## The Queen Of Dribble-Drabble

The Queen of Dribble-Drabble
Lives just down the hall from me.
She talks and talks and never stops,
Her lips move constantly.

She speaks what she is thinking,
But she never gives a thought
To whom she might be speaking to,
To whom she's maybe not.

The trip she took last summer,
A show she watched last night,
A something that a friend once said
That wasn't so polite.

Her plans for Sunday morning,
Or the sparkle of her ring,
The food she ate for lunch, today,
The songs she likes to sing.

The facts about her hamster,
All about her bandaged knee,
Her friend's new baby, puppy dog,
Or last year's Christmas tree.

It really doesn't matter,
Who is there or who is not.
The Queen of Dribble-Drabble Land
Just likes to talk a lot.

## Anecdote: *Fudge*

I don't remember who brought me the plate of fudge.  I do remember that one of my students, Melissa, very much wanted to have a piece of that fudge.  She kept asking for a piece.  Over and over.  It had turned into a classroom joke by the end of the day.  The following day I had the last say with **Fudge**.
Yes, I did sneak Melissa a piece of fudge as she left for home that day.... unnoticed by any of her classmates, naturally.

# Fudge

There's a fudge smudge
All over my face.
I love the smell,
I love the taste!

I'd have it for breakfast,
I'd eat it for lunch,
I'd like it for supper
If I had that much!

It tastes good when I'm happy.
It tastes good when I'm sad.
If you take my fudge away from me,
It can really make me mad!

Don't make me mad!

So, you'd better be careful, Melissa.
Don't think about touching this plate.
I'll give you a piece if you ask real nice.
If you don't, I'll procrastinate.

Forever!!!

## My Dad Forgot To Set the Clock

I know my hair's a tangled mess,
There's crusties in my eyes.
My unbrushed teeth
Don't smell so sweet,
I do apologize!

My tummy's growling way too loud,
My lunch pail's still at home,
My glasses, they're,
I don't know where,
Have you a pair to loan?

My shirt is put on inside-out,
My buttons front-side-back.
My shoes and socks
Are mixed, not matched,
I look a bit ransacked.

And breakfast was not put inside
The place it ought to be.
Inside my gut
My Cheerios,
Today are absentee.

My dad forgot to set the clock,
I got up late today.
And that is why,
You see that I,
Have come to school this way.

## *Anecdote:* Little Timmy

**DAY 1**

Kids are giggling.

"Okay. What's so funny?" I ask.

Silence.

"Really, something must be funny. You know I like funny."

Kimberly raises her hand.

"Mr. Fairley, haven't you noticed the ceiling?"

Looking up at the ceiling, I ask, "What's funny about the ceiling?"

"Can't you see it, Mr. Fairley?"

Still looking up. "No."

Giggling.

"Those little white things," Melissa says.

"*Oh*", I say."

Then I notice another little white thing, and another, and another, maybe a couple dozen little white things scattered across the ceiling....stuck to the ceiling.

"That's weird," I say. "Where did those white things come from? What are they?"

More giggles.

Then I get it. Spit wads.

"**Oh**!" I say.....

Smiling and chuckling, I ask, "How long have they been there?"

"A *long* time, Mr. Fairley." Bradley says.

Then laughing, I say, "I can't believe I've never noticed!"

More looking up. More laughing

Still laughing I say, "Okay, it's time to get back to work."

Teaching and learning resumes.

Later in the day I look up at the ceiling, chuckle again, and ask, "Who's responsible for all of this?"
Silence.
"Really, I'm impressed with this." I say.
I wait.
I'm on the hunt.
Finally, James says with a uncertain smile, "I did, Mr. Fairley."
I thank him for his response. With a puzzled look on my face, I ask "But when James?"
James is still smiling, "While you were writing on the board."
"Really?"
Still smiling, "Yes."
Then I wonder out loud, "But, how could just one person do all of this?"
"I didn't do all of it, Mr. Fairley." James clarifies.
"So, who helped you?" I ask.
James isn't sure what to say so he just sits there looking at his desk top and says nothing.
Tension enters.
My kids are now pretty sure where I've been going with all the smiles and compliments.
"Seriously," I repeat, "I really would like to know. This is remarkable!"
No response.
Silence.

Late in the afternoon I bring up the spit wad subject.

"Here's what I'm thinking about our ceiling," I say. "Give it some thought tonight. Maybe, tomorrow, you'll feel more like letting me know if you were one of James' helpers. Maybe drop a *little white* note on my desk."

## DAY 2

Next morning before recess I resume the conversation. "I didn't hear anything about our ceiling this morning. If you want, you can visit with me on your way to recess, if you have something to tell me."

No takers.

That's what I expected.

After lunch, I make a recommendation. "Might be a *good* idea to let me know if you were involved in the spit wad thing. You know that I *will* find out. And I think it would be *better* coming from you than from someone else."

Pressure mounts. I know that some of my kids are experiencing elevated stress levels.

My strategy is working as planned.

I'll wait a little longer. I find this entertaining!

## DAY 3

By noon the following day I have three more names. By the end of the day, a fifth and final name has been supplied. "Eric helped us," James says. "He asked us to tell you."

We do not talk about spit wads anymore that day.

All seems well. Everyone goes home with a cheery "good bye" from their teacher.

## DAY 4

The next day, I dismiss the class for morning recess, then I add, "Wait, I need to have the *spit wad team (SWT)* hang around. We need to talk. The rest of you, have a good recess."

I usually have a small group of kids at my desk immediately after the children are excused for recess. Questions, corrections, a little visiting, an attempt to get permission to stay inside for recess, etc. Teachers, aides, or parents may show up for one reason or another. I plan to use this reality as we resolve our spit wad incident.

During this first get together with the *SWT* we clarify the problem, who owns the problem, and who needs to resolve the problem. We're all on the same page.

I explain that I'm usually kind of busy during their recess, but that I'll do my best to find time to aid them.

"So, got any ideas about how to resolve this problem?" I ask. Silence.

"Well, we're out of time."

Recess is over. I suggest to SWT that we work on it during lunch recess.

It's lunch recess. The SWT is back. I encourage them to start talking.

To make a plan.

I give my attention to two children who are in to see me about some math that didn't get completed earlier. I check my plans for the afternoon. I watch SWT out of the corner of my eye. No sense of urgency over there.

Discussion turns to problem resolution. James tells me, "Mr. Fairley, we won't do it again." He's become the team spokesman. I respond, "I'm glad to hear that, James. Everybody agree?" Everybody agrees.

"So," I go on, "how do we clean up the ceiling?"

Blank looks.

Recess ends. Kids are coming into the room.

We know where to start next recess.

## DAYS 5-7

SWT comes up with many ideas as to how we might "de-spit-wad" the ceiling. When I find the time, I evaluate their ideas. Most are unsafe: using sticks (might break light bulbs), stacking desks (someone might fall), etc.

This goes on for a couple of days. Sometimes I fail to find time to connect with them and apologize profusely.

Finally the idea, "Ask the janitor to remove the spit-wads" comes up. We all agree that it would be the safe thing to do.

Another recess is over. I promise to ask the janitor if our idea will work for her.

## DAY 8

SWT is not out of the woods. I've got them where I want them. The janitor agrees to work with me. I tell SWT the good news. The janitor will be glad to help you out. Then I tell them the janitor wants to know what they can do for her. "After all, if she spends **her** time removing spit-wads from **our** ceiling, how will she get her work done?"

Puzzled expressions appear on the faces of five little guys who are very ready to join their classmates for a recess. "We'll figure that out next recess," I say.

An agreement is made. SWT will do work for the janitor. The janitor will remove the spit-wads from the ceiling. After eight long days, spit-wad removal begins.

SWT returns to recess, only needing to give the janitor one recess of work, each and separately. All SWT members have a good time working with the janitor.

During the whole process, I was able to portray myself as a sensitive, eager helper. There were no hard feelings or bad emotions. No complaining. No lecturing. No penalizing missed recesses. No talks with parents. Just problem solving. We talked about things not spit-wad. We expanded our relationship in new ways. It was as if I was a newly enlisted SWT member, enlisted for the singular purpose of helping them to resolve a not so small problem. Really, it was not a negative experience for SWT. It was very instructive.

Later in the year, we (our class), were trying to decide what we should do with a few spare minutes we had open. Suddenly, on impulse, I blurted out, with apparent excitement in my voice, "I know, let's shoot spit-wads at the ceiling." Without hesitation, five voices, in unison, returned an emphatic, "**noooo**".

So much fun for me!!!

The subject of spit-wads never came up again.

# Little Timmy

Little Timmy looked all around the room,
He was hoping for something to do.
So he asked a friend for his advice,
And his friend, he said, he knew,
Of a something fun, of a something cool,
That Timmy could do for a while.
And when Timmy heard his friend's advice,
Little Timmy began to smile.

Then, Timmy rummaged all through the stuff
He'd hidden inside his desk,
Till he found that thing he needed to make
His friend's advice work best.
And tearing a piece of paper from
His writing workbook page,
He was ready to put his plan to work
He was ready to engage.

Then winking his eye and opening wide,
Timmy popped that paper inside,
Then started to chew, and chewed some more,
Till a target he did spy.
And lifting his straw up to his lips
While taking a great big breath,
(Continued)

He sent a spit-wad flying toward
Little Anna Marie Macbeth.

Little Anna Marie was reading her book
When that spit-wad found its mark,
And it lodged inside her left side ear
Giving Anna Marie a start.
Then screaming out loud and jumping up,
She raced to her teacher's side,
"I think there's bug inside my ear,"
**"Please, help me, Please!"** she cried.

When teacher looked into Anna's ear
She was taken by surprise.
Instead of a bug hiding inside there,
A spit-wad's what she spied.
Then looking over toward Timmy's desk
To see what she might see,
She saw an expression of utter shock,
That cried out, **"It was me."**

Now, Timmy had spent a week inside,
Not outside with his friends.
When he asked his teacher if he could play,
She said, "It all depends."
So Timmy gave thought to what he had done,
To Little Anna Marie,
(Continued)

And he made the promise, "Never again,
Would he do such a cruel thing."

Well, time has passed, and come and gone,
And Timmy's a different kid.
He does not care for spit-wad fun,
But even if he did,
He'd aim to the left or he'd aim to the right,
He'd aim high or way down low.
How the wad he aimed at Anna's chair
Got in her ear, he doesn't know.

# Ouch

I stuck a note
On someone's back.

I watched.
I waited.
I smiled.

Ouch!
I feel a pain.
My bottom hurts.
Someone,
Has done the same!

# Anecdote: *Pocket Stuff*

Ms. Nancy notices that Jeremy keeps peeking into his pocket. She decides that she'll need to investigate.....when she finishes working with Aaron.

A few minutes later, Ms. Nancy looks up from Aaron's paper and glances around the classroom. Jeremy is peeking into his pocket, again. Thomas has joined him. Both boys are giggling. Ms. Nancy decides to give her full attention to observing Jeremy. She'll gather data.

Another child joins Jeremy and Thomas. Ms. Nancy decides it's time to intervene. Take a peek, herself. Gather data.

Ms. Nancy excuses herself, and walks over to the boys.

"So, Jeremy, whatever it is that you have, in your pocket, must be really interesting," Ms. Nancy remarks. Jeremy's smile fades. Thomas and his friend disappear to other parts of the classroom.

"Can I have a peek?" Ms. Nancy asks.

Jeremy shakes his head.

"What's in there, anyway?" Ms. Nancy persists.

No comment.

Ms. Nancy gives Jeremy an easy out. "Well then, Jeremy, do you think you can ignore whatever it is that's in there? Until recess?" Jeremy nods.

A few minutes later Ms. Nancy sees Jeremy and Thomas together, again. They're peeking into the pocket again. They're giggling, again.

Ms. Nancy already knows what she is going to do. She walks over to Jeremy and thrusts her hand down inside his bulging pocket.

Jeremy's face pales.

Ms. Nancy immediately recognizes the object in Jeremy's pocket…"It's a plastic snake." She is relieved. It's a **Simple** solution. She wraps her fingers around the plastic snake and extracts it from the pocket.

Something feels odd, to Ms. Nancy.

She realizes that the plastic snake is moving in her hand! Wriggling!

Writhing!

Ms. Nancy recoils in horror, flinging Mr. Garter Snake from her grip.

She screams!

Not a little scream!

Wriggling and writhing like Mr. Garter Snake, she struggles to regain her composure.

The classroom is silent.

Jeremy is in shock. He looks sick!

Ms. Nancy is in shock, too. Her face is pale.

Jeremy is ordered to retrieve Mr. Garter Snake and remove him from the classroom.

Ms. Nancy decides it's a good time to take the class to recess.

Ms. Nancy needs a recess.

# Pocket Stuff

There's lots of neat stuff
In this pocket of mine.
It's getting as full as can be.
With this and with that
I've found lying around,
With things that belong just to me.

This coin, bright and shiny,
I found on the street.
Its date is quite easy to read.
I bet it brings luck,
It was lucky of me,
To make such a find, yes indeed.

And, look at this rock,
It has speckles of gold.
Hey, check out this old rusty key.
I bet it would open
An old pirate's chest,
That's buried beneath an old tree.

Some gum and a nail,
And a short piece of string,
A crayon that's broken in two,
An old rabbit's foot

That's lost most of its fur,
A tooth, I on Sunday, outgrew.

There's lots of neat stuff
In this pocket of mine.
It's fuller than full, you'll agree.
I could show you much more,
But I haven't the time.
I've three pockets empty, you see.

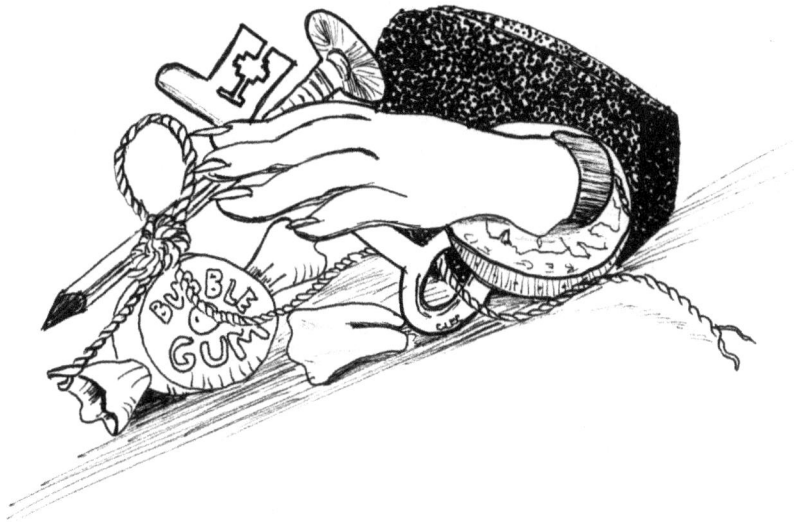

# Teacher's Point Of View

"Hey Teacher, please Teacher,
Give me your ear!"
From all around this classroom
That's all I can hear.
Children with questions,
Some children in tears,
Still others with play things,
All gathering near.

Sandy is angry
That John took her hat.
And Andy is holding
A little white rat.
Lee has a Pokémon,
Tyler a shell,
And Nikki has plastered,
Her hair full of gel.

Thomas is crying
His head off his neck,
And Sarah is moving,
She fears, to Quebec.
Ethan is hungry,
And Brittany feels sad,
Poor **Josh** needs to **go**,
And he needs to go bad!

Hey children! Listen!
It's my turn to plead!
Can I have a moment
To take care of me?
My brain is exploding,
My bladder has needs,
I'll be back in a moment
Hey **Josh**, Wait for me!

# I Won't!

I'd like to
But I can't.
I want to
But I don't.
I should,
I think.
I think
I shan't.
I could,
I would,
I won't!

So
Stop
Asking
Me!

# Doggy Stuff

Scoop up all the doggy stuff
Lying round the yard.
Drop it in a plastic bag,
It's really not that hard.
Toss it in the garbage can.
Push the lid down tight.
Don't you wish your puppy dog
Had manners more polite?

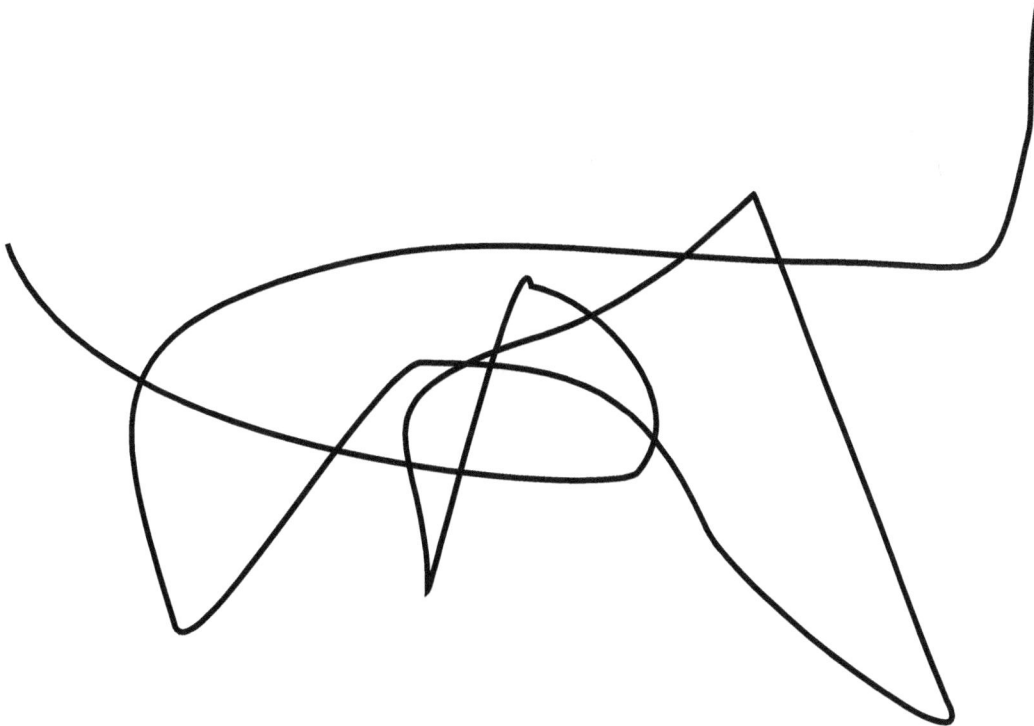

# Hair Spray

My older brother Jamie
Uses hair spray every day,
To stick his hair up in the air,
And keep it just that way.
And when he passes people
In the mall or on the block,
They stop to gaze and speculate
About his chic Mohawk.

My younger brother Tommy
Takes a slightly different tack.
He sprays his head until it's wet,
Then reaches for his hat.
And when his friends come over,
Or wind begins to blow,
His hat stays stuck right on his head
Like white sticks to the snow.

I have a somewhat different
Way of using spray each day,
To keep my pants from falling down
When I go out to play.
A little bit of hair spray
On my sitter-down place,
Does wonders with my baggy jeans
And saves me from disgrace.

# Dickory Dock

Hickory Dickory Dock,
A mouse, you say, ran up the clock?
Well, I've never heard tell.
Are you sure you feel well?
I fear you've gone Dickory Dock!

# Falling Down the Spout Can't Be All That Bad

As Eensy Weensy Spider
Crawled down the walk one day,
He spied a Robin Red-Breast
Just standing by the way.
"Hey, Mr. Robin Red-Breast,
Please tell me, if you please,
Where I may find a spout that I
Am sure to climb with ease."

But, Mr. Robin Red-Breast,
Without a word to say,
Devoured little spider,
Then went about his day.
And now, when rain clouds gather,
Though it may pour and pour,
The eensy weensy spider
Falls down the spout no more.

# Where in the Bathtub?

So, where in the bathtub,
Will Christopher sit?
Now that Christopher wants to
hop in.
He's loaded the tub
With his favorite stuff,
But, now there's no room left
for him.

A beach ball, a sponge,
And a long rubber snake,
A purple, inflatable frog,
Five blue, plastic fish,
And a small, yellow duck,
And a cute, little, live puppy
dog.

A wind-up speed boat
With a little, green man,
A high powered, super, squirt
gun,
Two G.I. Joe guys,
And a Pokémon dude,
And a model of Air Force One.

Now Christopher stands
With his snorkel in hand,
And he wonders just where he
will sit,
In a tub that's so grand
Stuffed with all he had planned,
But no place for his bottom to
fit.

# Turtle Soup

There's a turtle in my soup,
And he's waving up at me.
He's winking with a beady eye,
And snapping with his beak.
He's splashing and he's diving,
And now floating on his back,
As he nibbles and he chews
On a cauliflower snack.

Now he's jumping high and flipping,
Doing somersaults, midair.
Now slowly swimming round the bowl
Without a turtle care.
Since this turtle in my bowl's
Having so much turtle fun,
I think I'll let him have my soup
Until his turtle fun is done.

# Bubble Gum

Mark a page,
Mend a tear,
Stop a leak
That needs repair.
Seal a letter,
Make a print,
Blow a bubble,
Gather lint.
Stick a pencil
To a desk,
Pull a hair
Right off Dad's chest.
Keep a lunchbox
Closed so tight,
Add some balance
To a kite.
Fasten paper
To the wall,
Hold some clothes
Upon a doll.
Anything that
Needs to stick,
Bubble gum can
Do the trick!

# Grounded

Kate's sitting at the window,
Her friends are in the street.
They're playing tag and kickball,
She's grounded to her seat.

She thinks that if she only
Could change a thing or two,
She'd be out there beside them,
She'd laugh and play tag, too.

She'd kick the ball to Tori,
She'd ride her bike with Sue,
Or hide behind a tree trunk,
Then pounce and shout out
"**boo**!"

She'd maybe go to Gabe's house
To use his trampoline,
Or climb a tree with Michael,
Or play croquet with Jean.

But Kate is downright grounded,
Her future's looking dim.
She wishes she had never
Slapped her little sister Kim.

Wishing doesn't change a thing,
What's done is done, you see.
So Kate just sits and watches,
And longs to be set free.

# Baking

There's flour on Mariah's face,
There's chocolate in her hair,
And sugar crystals, small and white,
Are scattered everywhere.

There's egg shell pieces on the stove,
There's butter on the floor,
Vanilla stains the counter top,
And dribbles down a drawer.

A mixing bowl half filled with dough,
A spoon licked shiny clean,
Mariah's baking treats today,
Her very own cuisine.

# I Love Chocolate

Chocolate milk,
Chocolate malt,
Chocolate gummy bears,
Chocolate cake,
Chocolate shake,
Chocolate cream éclairs.

Chocolate pudding,
Chocolate frosting,
Chocolate covered nuts.
Chocolate toffee,
Chocolate coffee,
Chocolate coconut.

Chocolate turtle,
Chocolate pretzel,
Chocolate by the square.
Chocolate kiss,
Chocolate "Swiss",
Chocolate in my hair.

Chocolate chips by the bag are pretty good, too!

# Chores

My mom is always busy,
She has lots of chores to do.
She washes all the dirty clothes,
To make them look brand new.
She vacuums all the carpets,
Keeps the bathrooms fresh and clean,
And wipes those hard to get at spots
Where dirt and germs convene.
The kitchen is her big job,
All the spills and crumbs about,
The sink with all its greasy grime,
A royal mess, throughout.

My sister does the dishes
Every morning, noon, and night.
My brother has to sweep the floors,
And keep them looking bright.
And dad, he keeps the yard nice,
Pulls the weeds and cuts the grass.
He tidies up the garage each night,
And fills the cars with gas.

I know that I'm the smallest,
But I have a big job, too.
I'm the one that makes the messes,
And my job is never through!

# Banished

I've been banished to this
bathroom,
Till this bathroom's spic and span.
I can't play on my computer.
I can't play with my friend Ann.
Till the sink is clean and shiny,
Till the toilet scum is gone,
Till the smell inside the trash can
Doesn't smell at all so strong.
Till the mirror sparkles clearly,
Every image on its face,
Till the ring around the bathtub
Has all vanished without trace.
Till the floor is mopped and
polished,
Till the shower curtain's cleaned,
I'll be slaving in this dungeon,
I'm quite sure, till I'm eighteen!

# Jail Cell

I should have cleaned
My room last night.
I meant to, but oh well!
And now today,
I'm sad to say,
My room's my own jail cell.

# A Day at the Dentist's Office

Jed sat down on the dentist chair,
He was ready for the worst,
But the dentist, he just smiled at Jed,
Then he started to converse.

"I'm glad to see you here today,
It's a real nice day outside.
And it looks like it's been a real long time
Since I had a peek inside."

"So open wide, I'll look in there,
And don't mind this long syringe.
Does it hurt too much?  I hope you're fine.
Please try hard not to cringe."

Jed's lip grew numb as numb could be,
And his tongue he could not feel.
Then the dentist winked an evil wink,
And he grabbed his monster drill.

Jed closed his eyes and held his breath.
He prayed that drill wouldn't work.
Then he heard a whirring, whining sound,
And began to go berserk.
(Continued)

He shrieked a scream so loud and clear,
Then he jumped right off that chair,
And he tore around from room to room,
He was hoping to hide somewhere.

He found what he was looking for
In a closet dark and still,
Back behind a big box of dentist stuff,
Far away from that killer drill.
And then in the dark, to his dismay,
Heavy steps he heard draw near.
And they paused and stopped outside his door,
Jed was trembling in his fear.

He heard the door knob slowly turn,
A thin crack of light appeared.
Then Jed grew faint and then passed out,
Overcome by his own fear.

That's all young Jed remembers, now,
Of that frightful day in May.
And he wonders where his sore tooth went,
But his mom, well, she won't say.

# Yours, Rosemarie

I got a letter in the mail today,
A letter sent by me.
It asked how I was doing.
It was signed, "Yours, Rosemarie".

The letter told me I was eight years old,
And that I liked to sing.
It told me all about my
Pretty, silver, diamond ring.

The letter said my little sister, Grace,
Had lost her second tooth.
It said my favorite candy
Was a chewy Baby Ruth.

I even read about the Saturday
I visited the zoo,
And then about my little,
Very own, white cockatoo.

I learned a lot about myself today,
But nothing really new,
I think I'll write a letter back,
A letter to me, too.

# Nothing In The Mail Today

I got a nothing in the mail today,
That's not what I had hoped.
I was looking for a something,
For a package or a note.
A note that told me something critical,
Or shared a big surprise,
Or just asked how I was doing,
Before telling me goodbye.

And I'd be happy with an envelope
With money stuffed inside,
Or a notice notifying
That I'd won a major prize.
A little card from Uncle Jonathan,
A box from Gram and Gramps,
Anything from anybody,
Even Einstein or Rembrandt.

But there's exactly, only, not one thing
That's come for me today.
Has my mail for some strange reason
Ended up in San Jose?

# Kitty Cat

In the front door,
Out the back,
On the floor,
Then on my lap,
Purring softly,
Spitting mad,
That's just like
A kitty cat.

CLEE

# Grandma

There'll be no talks with grandma,
No cookies in the jar,
No stories of the olden days,
No tales from near and far.
No hand knit slippers crafted,
No quarters in her hand,
No candy coated peanuts,
No presents, oh so grand.

No pots of fresh cut flowers,
No playing in the yard,
No songs at the piano,
No happy birthday cards.
No busy days of canning,
No jars of applesauce,
No happy nights spent over,
No loving kisses tossed.

There'll be no memory making,
Only those already spun,
My grandma passed away last night,
My world just came undone.

# Stuck On Second Base

I hit the ball, I had to run,
I made it safe to first,
Then ran to second on a pitch
Way low down in the dirt.
And now I'm stranded way out here,
Far from the port-a-pot,
And trying hard to hold it in,
But fearing I cannot.

My knees are touching, pressing tight,
I'm doubled at the waist.
The pain inside is growing strong,
I don't think I can wait.
Now, "crack!" I hear my friend Jim's
bat,
Jim's running hard for first.
I'm going, too, but not to third,
My bladder just now burst.

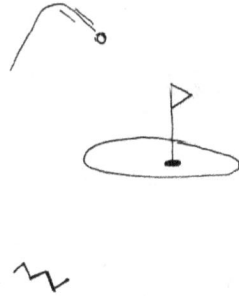

## Ostrich Sands

Ostrich Sands is quite the golfer,
With his long and limber neck,
He drives the ball with power,
With precision, and effect.
His chip is true and graceful,
And his follow through complete,
His putt is always perfect,
And his style is oh so sweet.

Ostrich Sands has recognition,
He's a real celebrity.
And people come from miles around,
To hear his golf club ping.
And he loves all the excitement
That his swing, so famed, creates,
And the fans that flock to see him,
And the game he dominates.

But each and every single night,
Before he goes to bed,
Ostrich needs to take two aspirin
To relieve his aching head.

# Eat Your Soup Dear!

This bowl of soup
You've given me,
Smells much too strong
Of Broccoli,
Of carrot, beet,
And Celery,
Of artichoke,
And black eye pea.

This bowl of brew
You've poured for me,
This pungent smelling
Soupy sea,
This murky mix,
This green cuisine,
Could not be good,
At all for me!

# Sting

I stooped to smell a flower
That was growing by the walk.
It wasn't much to ask,
One fragrant sniff,
That's all I took.

The honey bee
I did not see
Thought very, very differently!

# Bumblebee

The bumblebee
That flew at me,
The one that buzzed
So angrily,
The bee that left
It's mark on me,
Won't sting again,
I guarantee!

## Somebody Help Me (Fido's Sad Song)

There's a flea inside my collar,
And it makes me want to holler,
I hate that little, pesky, creepy crawler!

And the more I try to scratch him,
The more I just can't catch him,
And the more this situation grows more grim.

Won't you, please, somebody help me?
Stop this flea before it kills me!
Won't someone set this poor old doggy free?

# You'd Better Put Your Dog Inside

You'd better put your dog inside,
My cat's outside today.
She doesn't have much patience
For a doggy's kind of play.
She doesn't care for barking,
Or for jumping all around.
Fact is, she doesn't care for
Any kind of canine hound.

You'd better put your dog inside,
My cat can be real mean.
Last week she clawed a bulldog,
And the poor guy fled the scene.
I really need to warn you,
This is not a laughing thing!
If your doggy tries to pick a fight,
I will not intervene.

# At the Ice Cream Shop

Just look at all this ice cream!
I can hardly wait for mine.
I'm ordering a three scoop cone,
A cone of my design.

But look at all these flavors,
Mocha Fudge and Coconut,
Strawberry, Chunky Monkey, too,
And yummy Maple Nut.

There's Rocky Road and Tin Roof,
And there's Caramel Swirl Delight,
Some Triple Chocolate Chunk Divine,
Some Taffy Bit A Bite.

There's Chocolate Nut Fudge Brownie,
And some Sweet Pecan Praline,
Some Cookie Dough, some Bubble Gum,
Some real Vanilla Bean!

Forget about the cone, Ma'am,
One large bowl is what I need.
One scoop of each, that's what I'll take!
Yes, thank you, Ma'am, and please.

## Max

Max ran down to the water
With his boogie-board in hand,
And splashed across the shallows
Out to where the waves began.
Then lunging through the first one,
Landing belly on his board,
He kicked and paddled fiercely,
As the waves around him roared.

Each wave, as it approached him,
Raised him quickly to its crown,
Then, slipping right on past him
Left him sliding gently down.
One wave and then another,
Out to where they first appeared,
He paddled with a purpose,
Never glancing to the rear.

And then beyond the breakers,
Turning back toward the sand,
He waited for that big one,
For that wave that looked so grand.
He saw it in the distance,
Rising high above the rest,
An awesome looking sea swell
With some foam upon its crest.

Now Max was feeling nervous,
As that mighty swell drew near.
It loomed up high above him,
And his "nervous" turned to fear.
And then, as if by magic,
That great swell slid under him,
Then grew and grew beneath him,
Until Max was on its rim.

That wave rushed on with fury,
Frightened Max up on its crest,
His boogie-board beneath him,
His poor heart filled with distress.
The wind was blowing wildly,
Ocean spray flew in his face,
But Max clung to his purpose,
And he rode that wave with grace.
(Continued)

And then without a warning,
And not knowing what to do,
Max found that he was swimming
In a raging, churning brew.
He rolled and tumbled wildly,
Right side up, and upside down,
His mind raced in its panic,
He was certain he would drown.

And then as luck would have it,
That wild wave washed up on land,
And left the battered surfer
Sitting safely on some sand.
He sat there in the shallows,
With his board nowhere in sight,
And thought he might, just maybe,
Rather like to fly his kite.

# Anecdote: *Code Nine*

There's an odor in the air surrounding my desk. I become aware of it when I hear Kelly ask Alicia, "Do you smell what I smell?" This is followed by two simultaneous expressions suggesting olfactory distress.
I realize that I need a strategy. Quickly.

*Normally, if a little something slips out, unintentionally of course, I have a standard protocol. I blame it on one of the kids in the class. Most of the boys in my class think it funny to be caught red handed (bottomed), so it's usually not too much of a problem for anyone. "Wow," I"ll mutter preemptively, "That smells foul." I'll mutter this just loud enough for the kids sitting in the immediate area to hear. Then I'll walk off and let those kids work it out. No one claims responsibility so it always goes unsolved. If the kids in the "affected zone" get too loud (expressions of distress, accusations etc.), I'll bring relief to rising stress levels by saying something akin to "No big deal. We all let it slip sometimes. Give it a second. It'll drift away".*

On this particular day I face an interesting challenge. My protocol will have to be adapted. Alicia and Kelly are the only kids in the "affected zone". They're sitting in an easy chair.... behind my desk.... next to the window. No boys are near!
I can't think quickly enough. My stress level is rising and I fall back on the familiar. I employ standard protocol with one exception....no boys are present.

Alicia addresses me, " Mr. Fairley, can you smell that stinky smell".

 "What smell?" I ask.

"You can't smell it, Mr. Fairley?" Kelly says with a disdained look on her face.

"What does it smell like?" I ask.  Then, without waiting for an answer,

 I make a sour face and say, "**oh**!" while trying my best to fake innocence.

Am I believable? I wonder to myself.

Kelly and Alicia converse briefly and then Alicia asks, " Mr. Fairley, did you fart?"

"Of course not," I reply (lie).  Then I add, "Maybe it was Kelly." Bad move.

Kelly makes sure that both Alicia and I know that it wasn't her.

 I shrug, trying to perfect my innocent look.  I'm hoping and praying that this private discussion goes unnoticed by the rest of the class.

Kelly and Alicia converse again, very briefly...very, very briefly. As they climb off the chair and head towards their seats, Kelly mutters just loud enough for me to hear, and exactly loud enough that I won't **not** hear, "Mr. Fairley, **you** farted!"

The discussion never resumed, lucky for me!

Incidentally, I don't recall, ever again, seeing Alicia and Kelly snuggled together with their reading books......on **that** chair.

And, I can't help wondering if the incident came up when, presumably,  someone at home asked, "How was your day at school, today?"

*I was not brave enough to address this experience directly, as I did in *My Teacher's Breath*.  The boy in me did want to write something on the subject, so....*Code Nine*.

# "Code Nine"

Last Friday driving down the road
To visit Grandma Trent,
Enjoying all the sights we passed,
And feeling so content,
I sensed a sudden, pungent smell,
A strong ill-scented fume,
Then heard my father call "Code Nine!"
But not at all too soon.

My mother groaned, big sister shrieked,
My brother laughed out loud,
I rolled my eyes and turned my head,
And made a moaning sound.
In barely any time at all
The windows all were down,
Us choking, gasping, hanging out
As we drove right through town.

Then yesterday at half past ten,
While in a crowded line,
With grocery cart filled to the brim,
My sister croaked, "Code Nine."
Without a moment's slight delay,
We all abandoned ship.
We left our cart just sitting there,
Then thanked Sis for the tip.

And last week at the movie house,
Halfway into the plot,
The lady right in front of me
Did what she should have not.
We slid way down into our seats,
Then pulled our shirts up high,
Until they covered everything
Except our bulging eyes.

"Code Nine" is just a little phrase
My family puts to use,
To signal something's lurking near,
A something on the loose.
Of course there's more I'd like to tell,
But not right now, you see,
"Code Nine" is sounding all around,
I hope you'll pardon me!

# Leaves

The wind blew last night.
When I awoke,
I found she had swept the leaves
Neatly into the corner of the yard
Where the junipers grow.

Resisting was hard.
Just one jump,
Then into the bag.
That was my plan!

I hope the wind
Blows again
Tonight.

# My Brother Has the Chickenpox

My Brother has the chickenpox,
He gets them every day.
They last until he takes his bath,
And then they go away.

Some days they're red as pox should be,
Some days they're midnight blue.
Sometimes they're multi-colored pox,
It's strange, but yet it's true.

Today his pox are forest green
Except for on his nose.
The color there is violet blue,
And why do you suppose?

I'll tell you why those pox so few
Are colored shades of blue.
His forest green ran out of ink.
What else was he to do?